BECOME A
TRANSFORMATIONAL
ORGANIZATION

Galvanize agility without
losing stability to survive and
thrive the digital, disrupted,
and damaged world

A
SWITCH ON
BOOK

THRIVE YOUR FUTURE

Library of Congress Control Number: 2019945263

Jankel, Nick Seneca 1974–

Become A Transformational Organization:
Galvanize agility without losing stability to survive and thrive the digital, disrupted, and damaged world

First Edition, Oct 2019
Los Angeles, United States
Switch On Books
111 pp. incl. index

1. Organizational behavior, change and effectiveness.
2. Corporate culture 3. Leadership

Printed in the United Kingdom, United States
and wherever books are sold.

ISBN 978-1-9997315-4-0 (print book)
ISBN 978-1-9997315-5-7 (ebook)

Switch On Worldwide Ltd
London & Los Angeles

www.switchonnow.com

Discounts are available on quantity purchases by
corporations, associations, and others.

For details, contact the publisher through the website above.

ABOUT THE AUTHOR

Nick Seneca Jankel is a Cambridge-educated author, philosopher, professional keynote speaker, and transformation catalyst. He is the co-founder of a pioneering leadership, innovation, and organizational development enterprise and the chief architect of Bio-Transformation Theory, a methodology, process, and toolset for lasting transformation in any human system. Nick develops original thinking, powerful programs, and crucial tools that ensure leaders and individuals of all kinds can transform themselves and their organizations to thrive in the disrupted, digital, and damaged world.

Nick has worked with organizations as diverse as Nike, No. 10 Downing Street, HSBC, and Oxfam and has taught at many universities, including Oxford University, London Business School, SciencesPo (Paris), and Yale University. He has appeared in The Economist, The Guardian, and The Financial Times and obtained a Triple 1st Class degree in Medicine & History and Philosophy of Science from Cambridge University. Most of all he is a husband and father and loves nothing more than hanging out with his wife and two boys in a field, city, or festival.

OTHER BOOKS

Switch On: Unleash Your Creativity And Thrive With The New Science And Spirit Of Breakthrough

The Book of Breakthrough: How to Use Disruptive Innovation & Transformational Leadership To Create A More Thriving World For All

CONTENTS

INTRODUCTION

Over the last two decades, I have worked with scores of world-class organizations who, despite their differences in purpose, industry, products, business models, legal entities, and ownership structures, share a foundational challenge: how to design their organization to fit the fast-changing world and the intense evolutionary pressures it brings. From FMCG giants to pioneering non-profits, from global banking behemoths to massive public service providers, every organization we have engaged with is facing the evolutionary imperative with unprecedented intensity. It is adapt or die on an unimaginable scale. One S&P company is being replaced, on average, every two weeks.

By working to solve the adapative challenges with our clients, I have come to believe that most, if not all, of an organization's major problems, whether decreasing margins or a disrupted operating model, whether disengaged employees or a lack of agility, are actually symptoms of a much more profound issue: the blueprint upon which modern organizations are built is no longer a fit for the environment the organizations find themselves in. Because of this mismatch, as Yale School of Management estimates, 50-75% of the Fortune 500 will be extinct by 2027.

No enterprise is immune to evolutionary pressure and the forces of creative destruction which, faster than ever, are making every model obsolete, from conventional strategy planning to leadership competencies; from legacy IT systems to accreted expenses processes. The rapid acceleration of three foundational and pivotal "Triple Threats" is making this so: Exponential *digital* technologies that can scale innovative value propositions in months not decades. Seismically *disrupted* social systems with massively and rapidly changing customer needs and desires. And major ecological and psychological problems that are a direct result of our *damaged* world.

I believe that, to survive and thrive in this fast and furiously changing context, *every* enterprise, from small start-ups to multinational giants, must become Transformational Organizations: elegantly able to change what they do and how they do it to stay relevant as things change around them. A Transformational Organization continuously metabolizes changes in the outside world into concrete value within its boundaries, delivered through the constellation of activities that make up its business model(s). Until they lead the shift to a Transformational Organization, leaders will have to deal with endless and inexhaustible crises that cannot be truly resolved, as opposed to temporarily fixed, using conventional management science, and management practices that evolved to control Industrial-Age, as opposed to Digital Age, organizations.

In this powerful yet short book, I suggest that, because the very blueprint of the modern organization is maladapted to the future, the solution for how to ensure your organization can cope with the digital, disrupted, and damaged world cannot be another restructure or change program based on the same Industrial-Age blueprint that created the problems in the first place. Instead, every leader has to transform the *source code* of organization itself into one that fits the Digital Age.

Through my deep inquiry and innovation in this space—which is very much a work in progess as I explore "organization" past and possible—I believe my team and I have begun to unfold an answer: transforming the blueprint we use to architect and structure organizations from a Command and Control hierarchy into a "Create & Control" system. Create & Control fuses the *generative* best of hierarchies with the *creative* best of self-organizing teams within networks. At the heart, Create & Control is an actively managed dynamic tension between adaptability (creativity and innovation) and stability (control and efficiency).

This is a fundamental transformation in the very blueprint upon which your enterprise is built. Because of this, there can be no one-size-fits-all solution to how to become a Transformational Organization built on a Create & Control blueprint. Agile software techniques, training programs, and even digital transformation projects alone will not do it. There is, however, a *process and toolset*—that we have curated over 20 years at the cutting-edge of change—for how to transform your organization systematically and strategically. We call this The Transformation Curve.

This book seeks to start you on your journey across The Transformation Curve so you can unleash the creativity, agility, purpose, and passion that lies latent in your people—*and which you need to* safely *harness right now* in order to forge the future, rather than fail it.

CHAPTER 1.
THE JOYS OF THE MODERN ORGANIZATION

The modern organization is an incredible thing. It allows us to come together to realize unprecedented bold and ambitious visions with minimal transaction costs. It has enabled human beings to work together to achieve stunning outcomes, such as the global spread of antibiotics; victory in world wars; the worldwide distribution of the personal computer; and the creation and distribution of digital apps for just about every practical need.

Modern organizations are fascinating: They are legal entities in their own right, although they are made up of individuals. They have a unique and often persistent culture, but it is a crystallization of the feelings, fears, beliefs, assumptions, and habits of each person who has ever worked in them. They create our thoughts, but we create theirs. They can be designed, managed, and led with full accountability; but they can never be totally controlled, try as we might.

In the heyday of the hierarchical organization, the massive concentration of resources enabled by hierarchy—human, industrial, technological, financial capital—allowed massive projects to be realized, from the pyramids to the iPhone, with clear accountability and enormous efficiencies of scale. The costs of doing business—people making and selling stuff—were reduced, allowing for unprecedented investment in innovation, both private and public. Whether we think of the East India Company or Bell Labs, the large modern organization—underpinned by Command & Control hierarchical structures and management techniques—worked to amass incredible wealth, deliver at huge scale, and drive mass-produced products and services into ever-expanding global markets.

When access to the means of production and distribution was limited, and most citizens were not empowered politically or psychologically, the modern hierarchical organization was an accurate fit to the world. Whether making and airing TV shows, printing and selling books, discovering and mainstreaming chemicals, or building and popularizing railways and skyscrapers, only those with access to huge amounts of capital—which could be wielded efficiently by hundreds of willing workers—could play. Large hierarchical organizations, leveraging capital from investors or taxpayers, were the only organizing systems capable of making and selling advanced innovations profitably and productively.

The elemental purpose of the modern organization—to maximize the outputs of Industrial-Age innovations—needed a management "science" to make it. Pioneered by firms like General Motors in the 1920s, the tools and techniques were designed to optimize the production line. Inspired by the relatively easy optimization of machines, a vast body of mechanistic thinking about organization development, structures, operational models, financing, auditing, accounting, quality and improvement, hiring and firing, revenues and performance management, emerged. The purpose of almost all of it was to increase efficiencies, reduce waste, and expand profits/productivity. The modern organization fashioned the world in its own Industrial-Age image: a humming, efficient machine.

This machine-focused, Industrial-Age thinking, often called Taylorism after management scientist Frederick Taylor, is now the "best practice" taught on MBAs and in management training programs from Lagos to London Business School. It is replete with machine metaphors like "efficiency", "outputs", and "productivity".

Spreadsheets, databases, P&L statements, Gantt charts, customer segmentation, engagement surveys, and more, whilst useful in many ways, all attempt to corral complex, messy, contradictory human beings ("human capital", the "supply chain", "customer segments"), into tidy boxes that can be measured and tweaked for increased productivity/profitability. Such organizational technologies have attempted to shape society into the neat linear forms of the production line.

Such hierarchical management techniques and technologies have had a brilliant impact on scale, efficiencies, and, sometimes, excellence. But they also crush creativity, humanity, and authenticity, as millions have discovered. The story of how Ray Kroc took the

McDonald's brothers' home-spun innovations in burger quality, customer service, and kitchen order and turned them into an Industrial-Age behemoth, elegantly brings this to life. My first job was as a burger-flipper and fry-maker at an outpost of this enormous empire. Here I experienced first-hand absolute hierarchy in management; and the alienating and dehumanizing nature of the modern organization when taken to extremes.

Although such large-scale hierarchical environments have never been a truly ideal environment for employees to thrive in, the low expectations of workers for autonomy, purpose, creativity, community, and collaboration meant that for a few centuries, large hierarchical organizations were able to be successful, despite their obvious weaknesses as employers. They have succeeded for so long because society was relatively static, and people were generally disempowered. You were lucky to get a job in a big organization: it was reasonably safe, relatively supportive, and you were paid a fair wage (with some obvious exceptions).

The grounding assumption was that a modern organization could expand and grow into new markets without limits because planetary constraints and other "externalities" were little understood or conveniently ignored; and people believed that the nature of modern life would not change that much so modern hierarchical organizations would be fit for purpose forever.

The social contract of the last century was premised on the ideal that hard work in a decent job in a stable organization allowed people to afford a home, a car, and a middle-class life. The alienation of mechanization and the suffering of hierarchy were tolerated because the end justified the means (for most). Periodically during the Industrial Age, people fought back against the mechanizing tendencies of the modern organization: whether in John Ruskin's *Unto This Last* (that inspired the birth of the Labor Party in the UK and Gandhi's activism in India); or by rebelling against *The Organization Man* of William Whyte—a suited, booted, usually male manager who succeeds by playing by the rules. But there were few genuine alternatives. So the Industrial-Age, hierarchical organizational paradigm of Command & Control has persisted both economically and socially.

Until now, that is.

CHAPTER 2.
COMMAND & CONTROL SYSTEMS

In order to transform a system, we must first understand it. So let's penetrate to the hidden order of Command & Control systems, particularly key underlying assumptions, to help us know what to transform and why. None of this is "right", but a useful exercise in identifying the formative drivers of systems we want to change:

Overall Goals

To maximize predictable returns on often substantial investment using hierarchical/"vertical" power, economies of scale, and efficient production processes to constantly improve performance/efficiency. Control, invariance, and stability are valued; creativity and agility discouraged.

Value Creation

The (incremental) improvement of products/services that serve customer needs along with the constant reduction of costs. Products and services are marketed to generally disempowered customers/users to generate demand for ever-increasing supply/efficiencies. Vertically-integrated business models/supply chains harness efficiencies of scale to maximize profits.

Ownership & Financial Returns

Ownership is given to those with invested capital. Returns are maximized by the accumulation, extraction, and abstraction of profit. Within the organization, ownership flows to those with the most ambition/talent, education/class advantages, and hierarchical power. Meritocracy sees those at the top as more valuable and to be rewarded as such.

Accountability & Authority

Goals are directed by accountable managers with vertical power to sanction, correct, and reward performance. KPIs are set, measured, benchmarked, and tracked to maintain accountability. Organizations favor KPIs premised on stability/improvement even when engaged in agility/innovation, which stifles transformation. Line managers surpervise reports within functional business units ("silos") to maintain order and control.

Visual Metaphor

A pyramid with employees at the bottom serving the senior managers and shareholders at the top.

FIGURE 1 Dominative Hierarchies

In a conventional hierarchy, those at the bottom serve those at the top, rather than customers (often attempting to guess what those with most vertical power want). Those at the bottom feel disempowered and disengaged whilst those with most vertical power often enact a "tyranny from the top" whether consciously or not.

Roles

Roles are designed by managers/HR and concretized into job descriptions that are updated infrequently. People have little chance to adapt roles without formally applying for new roles. Roles are often designed to serve legacy processes and the management of existing business models as opposed to serving emerging customer needs, transformation, and innovation.

Responsibilities

A culture of fear and «being right» prevents elegant and clear responsibility-taking. Responsibility is seen as a moral question of whether someone is right/wrong or good/bad rather than an empowering way of owning problems, and so their solutions, creatively.

Guidance & Decision-Making

Explicit rules to guide behavior and decision-making are generated by managers and issued within policies, protocols, and contracts. The rules tell people what to do and how to do it to stay legal/compliant and «right» in accordance with what managers believe best practice is. Failure to comply are penalized, often with punishment. There are also implicit rules, expectations, and agendas that remain hidden. Guessing and serving agendas wastes much of the discretional energy and effort of team members. Behavior modification is focused on individual performance gaps rather than using errors and issues to ensure the organization's ruling assumptions are challenged if they are out-dated and ready for disruption.

Processes

Unwieldy processes, usually generated by managers and consultants, accrete over time to control outcomes. Many legacy processes and policies still operate without strategic design; they were created in reaction to new legislation and/or failures and generate much friction, frustration, and waste.

Key Activities

Manage the existing business/people according to best practice. Sales/marketing to create customer demand. Efficiency and technology upgrades deployed to reduce costs/boost productivity. Mergers/aquisitions to boost scale/growth and to defend competitive advantage. HR/IT/Finance (etc.) functions support.

Innovation

If it occurs, it is focused on relatively risk-free incremental improvements. Innovation programs are run top-down and often fail to challenge the dominant rules of the industry due to management groupthink/groupfeel. Transformation and disruptive innovation are blocked.

Motivational Levers

Focus on extrinsic motivation: Rules and rewards (promotions, recognition, awards, bonuses, share options) which rapidly diminish in effectiveness.

Culture

Risk averse, anti-disruptive groupthink/groupfeel, and blame/shame/complain cultures minimize transformation. People look busy and get stuff done with little space, time, or permission for reflection, connection, and co-creation.

Diversity

Ensure everyone 'salutes the flag', minimizing variation and dissent whilst complying with diversity compliance.

Information Flow

Managed communications cascade information and instructions from top to bottom with a bias towards under-communication and secrecy.

Leadership

Formal hierarchy according to management position with a bias towards heroic, technical, and/or feudal (within "silos") leadership styles. Employees tend to serve the needs (explicit or implicit) of people with vertical power rather than what the customer needs. Senior leaders believe they must be the smartest people in the room.

Coaching & Empowerment

Feedback on blind spots is not welcomed, particularly by senior management. People tend to blame/shame/complain rather than take responsibility. When coaching and empowerment occur, managers conflate difficult management conversations with genuine coaching and empowerment.

Organizing Principles

Linear mechanistic thinking in the form of production processes and operational algorithms attempt to predict outputs and control messy human behavior. Products are standardized and processes optimized. Technology is sought to replace costly human labor. Data and knowledge are valued above insight and intuition in order to predict/control human behaviour and so profits.

Underlying Assumptions About Human Nature

People are inherently unable, unwilling, and untrustworthy and need to be controlled and directed to be productive and efficient. Some are inherently more valuable than others.

CHAPTER 3.
THE NEW REALITY

The world is going through a fundamental change in its deep code or Operating System (O.S.). The "Triple Threat"—exponential digital technologies, disrupted societies (radical changes in the needs and expectations of consumers and producers), and existential risks to our survival from our damaged psychological and ecological systems"—challenges *every* organization to adapt their design and structure to survive it, let alone thrive in it.

Characteristics of The Digital Age

- Exponential technologies that can scale rapidly by being adopted and adapted easily

- Driven by the web, but much more than it: from ecosystem business models to co-working spaces

- People connect with each other in unprecedented ways, allowing new possibilities to emerge

- Information / money / people move
  with far fewer boundaries, changing our
  societies and challenging our systems

- Value increasingly becomes distributed to the
  edges: power, insight, creativity—with associated
  political, economic, and civic turbulence

- Peer-to-peer, sharing and
  disintermediation abound

According to research done by the Rand Corporation, the digitally inspired network-driven Operating System that is emerging in our shared reality is an unprecedented stage in the development of human culture. In fast-changing and fluid web, ideas, data, money, and sometimes people, move around networks with blinding speed. As a result, customers and consumers often get smarter, and wiser, faster than organizations can respond.

Whereas for centuries the environment we had to operate within was stable, predictable, familiar and clear, it is now volatile, uncertain, complex, ambiguous; VUCA for short. This makes traditional strategy and planning techniques woefully inadequate.

Whereas the strong, powerful, and competitive, won in the past, in the world of digitally inspired networks, the co-creative thrive. In a digital ecology, power is relentlessly pushed away from the fiefdoms and silos of the Industrial Age. Inspired and rewired by the web, power is flung to the edges: coders, blockchainers, leading-edge hipsters and hackers, fringe voters, and disruptive innovators.

Here, weak ties across a wide network, are more powerful for innovation and success, than close ties within your organization.

As the cost of manufacturing and distributing products and services has dropped, and digital technologies and techniques have become increasingly commodified, pretty much anyone can launch a disruptive innovation and topple an Industrial-Age giant. In the Digital Age, today's disappointed and smart customers can easily become tomorrow's empowered, exponential entrepreneurs.

Companies born with digital technologies at their core can scale faster, innovate quicker, and deliver cheaper, than legacy Industrial-Age organizations can, thus leading to the disruption of industrial business models and the organizations that embody them.

Disappointed Customers Become Visionary Disruptors

Travis Kalanik, founder of Uber, was trying to hail a cab in Paris one night. It was a difficult thing to accomplish, yet cars were passing by every second that were empty. Kalanik, with no car industry experience or resources, realized that he could solve a global market fail with transformational innovation. Uber is now worth more than GM, Ford or BMW, all Industrial Age business models and organizational systems.

Digital is just one element of the "Triple Threat". Seismic and highly disruptive shifts in human expectations are being driven by (and also driving) the digital technology. People are more and more "woke", expecting equality, empowerment, and ethics in the workplace as a hygiene factor. They want brands that can offer them the same. The demand for meaning, membership (community and connection), and mastery (autonomy and enablement) is making old levers of motivation and desire increasingly irrelevant.

Since the 1970s, real wages have been dropping (a 30% drop since 2008 for UK workers alone). Jobs have steadily becoming more meaningless whilst workers have become more aware of the value of purpose and fulfillment. Voters are feeling the pain of lowering standards and reduced dignity. They are voting in populists and demagogues as a result. One in four Europeans voted for a far-right party in the last string of elections. This has precipitated a major social crisis about the underlying social contact, whose symptoms can be seen in recent political upsets.

At the same time, we are facing existential risks to our species' ability to live successfully on this planet. From Greta Thunberg to Al Gore, from striking school kids and doctors calling for nonviolent civil action to the success of plant-based burgers, people are realizing rapidly just how quickly we might be approaching an extinction event: our own. This does not even count the issues we face with pollution, biodiversity and pollinator losses, the obesity and anxiety epidemics, and the simple lack of clean water and fertile soil.

CHAPTER 4.
THE PAIN OF THE MODERN ORGANIZATION

To understand the extent of the challenges that the "Triple Threat" (digital, disrupted, and damaged drivers of change) offers modern organizations, it is crucial to be aware of the cybernetic Law of Requisite Variety, also known as Ashby's Law. The Law states that an organism/organization must have the same level of variety within it as is found in the external environment it exists in. In other words, an organization can only cope with the spectrum of challenges that arise in its ecosystem if it has a palette of responses which are as varied and creative as the problems it must solve.

In static, and statist, markets, an organization does not need much variety—diversity, inclusion, empowerment, creativity, purpose, innovation, co-creativity etc.—within to succeed. In fact, the Industrial Age exploded into every home *because it reduced variety* on the production line so that every box of cereal or porcelain plate was identical to any other. Standardization of sizing and components was vital to scaling once-prohibitively expensive products and services to billions of people. "Variance" was eliminated from production lines. But variance is another term for thinking differently and adapting in real time.

Put simply, the command and control hierarchy evolved *precisely to prevent the agility and adaptability necessary to survive in today's digital, disrupted, and damaged economy.* The world is massively more varied and complex than it was even twenty years ago. So Industrial-Age organizational theory and practice that limits variance, creativity and agility is leading most modern organizations to fade; and many to fail: they are becoming increasingly irrelevant and so under-performing, given their abundant access to different forms of capital.

Signals That An Organization Is Fading . . . And Failing The Future

- Immense focus on boosting accounting profits over innovating value-creating propositions

- Reliance on commodifying products and services

- Enormous efforts made for marginal gains

- Out-dated business models disrupted by more agile and value-creating upstarts

- Accretion of control-centered processes causing friction and frustration

- Steep hierarchies limiting innovation at the edges, where new customer needs and problems are discovered

- Need to grow through expensive acquisitions and ineffective mergers

- Lack of genuine cognitive and ethnic diversity and equality

- Defending markets with lobbying instead of adapting

- Unserved customer needs, creating constant churn and unresponded to complaints

- Unserved employee needs leading to retention and attraction issues

- Learned helplessness crippling effectiveness and agility

- The ideas and insights of juniors are ignored, causing disenfranchisement

- Sidelining of genuinely creative thinkers as "mavericks"

- Lack of shared and authentic purpose to serve society

The Industrial-Age organization, with Command & Control systems at its core, is no longer working optimally in the digital, disrupted, and damaged reality. It is struggling to keep major enterprises competitive and innovative in the marketplace—and attractive places for employees to spend the majority of their time and energy.

The Command & Control companies of today are hierarchies where all efforts are focused on serving the needs of the CEO and the shareholders he/she must placate. They quickly become dominative, with toxicity and tyranny cascading down from the top, even if nobody consciously wishes to dominate their fellow humankind. This is causing profound failures across every measure of success.

In economic terms, most large organizations no longer invest in, or can deliver, genuine transformational innovation. Research has shown that the organizations that have the most traditional market power, actually spend *less* on R&D than others. Innovation falls as industrial concentration increases. What this means is that most large, hierarchical, and linear organizations no longer compete on innovation at a time that most are being disrupted by more innovative and agile competitors.

Even the International Monetary Fund has warned in 2019 that the size and power of the large tech companies are reducing innovation overall as these companies use mergers and acquisitions to remove competitors, leading to an increase in prices for customers and profits for the businesses.

Many studies have shown that as an organization gets older and larger, it becomes far less innovative. The funding for innovation lags the spending on bureaucracy as the organization employs more people to manage—to command and control—others. Geoffrey West, a professor who researches size and scale relationships in complex systems, discovered that "all large mature companies have stopped growing." Hierarchical organizations reach a point where their growth becomes massively *bounded* by their own commanding and controlling natures. Chris Argyris from Harvard Business School believed that hierarchical structures turn people into needy, passive, disempowered, conforming human beings that limit innovation and growth.

Most of the processes and policies in a Command & Control system have accreted over time. This has not been driven by smart human-centered design to enable creativity and mass empowerment to serve changing user needs but to curtail such distributed leadership in the first place. This has been an understandable, but problematic, *reaction* to legislation, litigation, management fads, "failures", and internal crises. Over decades such processes and procedures have become "barnacles" that create tremendous organizational drag and entropy. Research has shown that drag from maladaptive processes robs organizations of as much as 25% of their "output": maladapted expenses processes are the biggest thieves of lost productivity. Other research has shown that over 80% of leaders are maladapted to the "Triple Threat" (the digital, disrupted, and damaged world), making the average organization half as productive as it should be.

Groupthink (and groupfeel) cascades from top to bottom from managers who achieved reputational and financial success in the closing decades of the Industrial Age. This, along with friction from Byzantine "matrix" structures, drag from hidden power dynamics and agendas in the hierarchy, and treacle-like processes that block decision-making, together rob people of the sense of forward momentum they need to feel good at work; and robs the organization of its innate innovation potential.

The Industrial Age paradigm assumes that the world is linear: a dead yet predictable algorithm rather than a living and unpredictable organism. This tendency to control human beings as if they were machines is fast-becoming maladaptive, particularly as organizations are waking up to the realization that they *need* those same human beings: not just to tweak the production line (an AI will do this better than humans can) but to innovate to compete against leaner, more creative, and more disruptive competitors.

Faced with ever-diminishing competitiveness and productivity, and a lack of innovation effectiveness, large organizations have been forced into expensive and risky acquisitions (and mergers), few of which have paid off for the buyer or the seller (let alone the user, deprived of genuinely new ways to solve their pain points). They could have created the transformational innovations they need for a fraction of the cost.

Command & Control Companies Forced Into Expensive & Defensive Acquisitions & Mergers

Unilever bought *Dollar Shave Club* in 2016, a start-up founded in 2011 by a pair of entrepreneurs who were frustrated by the cost of razor blades. This duo raised relatively small amounts of funding at first, around $1 million. Unilever bought them for $1 billion (that's 1000 million dollars) just 5 years later. That is an "exponential" return of 1000x to the founding investors. The company sells razor blades, that they don't even manufacture themselves, on the internet surrounded by lifestyle content. This is truly a model of the Digital Age.

The founders did not have anything like Unilever's resources; but they had lashings of creativity and agility. Unilever could have easily generated this innovation—and hundreds more like it—at a fraction of the cost of the aquisition but didn't precisely because of *hierarchical* management and structure that prevents disruptive ideas from being entertained. I am sure that various employees of Unilever had an idea similar to Dollar Shave Club in the 5 years before they acquired the start-up. But Command & Control systems are designed to block such "risky" variance/innovation.

To protect their interests, instead of innovating, large organizations often lobby for rules that allow them to become virtual monopolies, as in the consolidated airline industry (United we stand) and the online search business (Google does no evil).

Organizations that cling to Industrial-Age principles and management theories are struggling to attract, motivate, develop, unlock, and retain the most creative, high-quality, transformational people. This shows up throughout their organizational culture and in their success metrics. Every human being in the networked global system is becoming ever-more awake and woke: vendors, consumers, investors, and workers. People are no longer entirely content to exist for the majority of their lives in small cubicles, dedicating 10 hours a day to dubious goals and the promotion of profit for a very few.

Dissatisfaction is rife. Creativity is down. Retention is challenging. Productivity is dropping. People within dominative hierarchies driven by command and control management become less inspired, less empowered, and less creative. Given that an inspired employee has been found to be 125% more productive than a satisfied one, this is a fundamental challenge to effectiveness *and* efficiency.

The complexity of the "Triple Threat" of existential risks, disrupted customer needs, and exponential technologies in the "metamodern" landscape requires the genius of many hearts and minds to come together to develop and deliver transformational solutions. The non-linear, fast-changing systemic connectivity of today is way too complex for linear, hierarchical organizing systems alone to cope with.

In networks, no one person, including the CEO or President, can understand even a fraction of the complex web of suppliers, technologists, data centers, distributors, retailers and customers that make up the organization they manage/lead. They certainly cannot adapt products and services in real time to respond to rapidly changing consumer needs and technologies. Which is why many of our organizations and systems—private, public, and political—are no longer creative, agile, and networked enough to survive, let alone thrive.

Nothing less than a complete transformation of the blueprint of "the organization" is enough.

CHAPTER 5.
FROM DOMINATIVE TO
GENERATIVE HIERARCHIES

Given their lack of innovativeness and competitiveness, hierarchical organizations must have a paradigm shift to better fit the "Triple Threat" of the digital, disrupted, and damaged world. This begins with a transformation in the underlying nature of the hierarchy that runs through them. Rather than be premised on domination of those at the bottom to serve the needs of those at the top, we need to move towards *generative* hierarchies that leverage the intelligence and wisdom of those with accountability to serve those who deliver excellence for customers.

Unlike some, such as those promoting Teal Organizations, Holocracy, and DAOs (Decentralized Autonomous Organizations), our extensive practical experience *and* our understanding of human behavior shows us that hierarchy in itself is not entirely dead. Far from it. We need hierarchies to afford systemic thinking and deliver transformational, as opposed to incremental, innovations. In fact, Paul Cilliers, a Professor of Complexity, states in his paper *Boundaries, Hierarchies and Networks in Complex Systems* that "systems cannot do without hierarchies . . . for them to exist at all there has to be some form of hierarchy."

The "Triple Threat" of the digital, disrupted, and damaged reality requires us to include useful control-oriented management skills and tools *but also transcend their very obvious limitations.* This means getting a lot smarter *and* wiser about how we design, manage, lead, and guide the hierarchies we are part of—and this does not mean buying some beanbags, doing some engagement surveys, and offering free coffee.

For hierarchies to fit with the new reality, they must be adaptable from within. This is rarely achieved with a re-org or re-structure driven by cost-cutting urges. As Professor Cillier goes on to say that "part of the vitality of a system lies in its ability to transform hierarchies. Although hierarchies are necessary in order to generate frameworks of meaning in the system, they cannot remain unchanged. As the context changes, so must the hierarchies."

To allow hierarchies to adapt, leaders must unleash the human potential for transformation that lies dormant in every organization. Leaders must authentically move away from "dominative hierarchies" that engender toxic forms of leadership (tyranny from above) within rigid power structures underpinned by calcified roles. These block transformation. They must turn towards generative hierarchies that support people to step up, adapt, and deliver excellence where it is needed most: at the point where the business solves the problems of customers that the users cannot solve themselves.

Whereas dominative hierarchies are inward-looking and governed by Command & Control systems where most efforts go towards pleasing the boss (and guessing how to do that much of the time), generative hierarchies are customer-focused, led by transformational leaders who understand how to use their power, influence, and intelligence, to bring the best out of their teams and the organization's resources as a whole, in order to generate value for their users. Accountability, motivation, and control mechanisms are all used sparingly, and only when absolutely necessary, to help shape generative outcomes for customers.

Generative Hierarchies in Healthcare

The new CEO of Lakeland Health discovered that his healthcare organization, with about 4,000 employees, suffered from low scores in customer (patient) satisfaction despite many initiatives to improve the metrics. The CEO realized there was a systemic issue: the organization's purpose was not coming through to the patients. He wanted to invert the pyramid and support the vital front-line associates to delight service users, not the boss.

So the CEO went on the road to engage the team, telling them to "Bring your heart to work: Every time you interact with a patient, tell them who you are, what you're there to do, and then share a heartfelt way." Within 90 days, patient satisfaction had jumped from the bottom c. 25% to the top 95th percentile for the first time ever. As the CEO states: "Beyond the improved satisfaction score, there was a clinical benefit. When we touch the hearts of our patients we create a healing relationship that generates a relaxation response, lowers the blood pressure, improves the happy neurotransmitters, reduces pain, and improves outcomes — for both the patient and the caregiver."

In a generative hierarchy, those at the "top" do not merely issue edicts and make tough decisions but *help the organization think in profoundly systemic, complex, and innovative ways.* Rather than pretend everyone is equal, we want leaders to be more "developed" and so more systemic thinkers and more able to find clarity in complexity (for more on this, see the developmental theory of Lawrence Kohlberg or the *Model of Hierarchical Complexity* put forward by M.L. Commons and others.) Such leaders are paid to develop their capacity to think and act in complex ways without anyone ever thinking they are "better" people.

We want senior leaders to achieve advanced stages of cognitive complexity, so they can engage with the radically complex VUCA work and crack transformational challenges with strategic brilliance and profound insight. We want them to have reached a stage of development akin to the "self-transforming" mind of Harvard developmental psychologists Robert Kegan and Lisa Lahey. But we don't want them to "get high on their own supply" and think they are more important or inherently valuable human beings.

Generative hierarchies need senior leaders who are not just smart and successful, moving up the stages of cognitive complexity; but also wise, emotionally mature and courageous. They must take up neither too little nor too much space. They must have what I call advanced "affective-interoceptive complexity" or "embodied wisdom" for short: able to handle the fear, chaos, and confusion inherent in the VUCA world without becoming protective and defensive.

Leaders in generative hierarchies need not just a sharp mind to simplify complexity for strategic decision-making and to envision and deliver transformational innovations that generate exponential value. They also need what I call a healed heart which allows them to support their teams to deliver with empathy and care without needing (all) the praise, power, or profit. They must be prepared to be ultimately accountable for the organization's performance through control mechanisms without being needlessly controlling, unless it truly is in the interests of all. They must take responsibility for mistakes without taking things personally. Above all, they must be always ready to relinquish their outdated behavioral patterns (like micromanaging, cynically diminishing others, or constantly kiboshing other people's ideas) to genuinely empower others. This takes a lot of conscious, purposeful, and creative leadership.

Dominative hierarchies usually contain many wounded egos running amok in positions of power, uncritically using outdated technical thinking to try and solve new transformational challenges, whilst directing an all-out drive for efficiency and (often personal) success no matter the human cost.

Research shows that such managers have a long term negative impact on motivation and cooperation, both massively important in the Digital Age. Generative hierarchies tend to be driven by people who have transcended their need to seem smart, powerful, or to be obeyed and who are therefore free to use all their hard-won and often specialist skills to support their teams to solve complex systemic and adaptive challenges, storytelling, inspiring, and transforming conflicts along the way.

Rather than the typical pyramid of hierarchy with those at the bottom (whether "labor" or "subordinates") serving those at the top—the managers and investors— the generative hierarchy looks like an inverted pyramid. Those with most old-fashioned vertical power, managers, board members and stockholders at the core of the company, understand that their role is to serve those who actually solve customer need. Senior leaders do not need to be the smartest in the room but instead know how to leverage technical genius—about AI or climate change— in creative, innovative, and transformational ways to deliver new forms of value to the customer.

The senior managers who form the apex (now bottom) of the inverted pyramid share and clarify the vision of the organizations and help those at the base (now top) do their jobs with as little noise and confusion, and as much agency and responsibility, as possible.

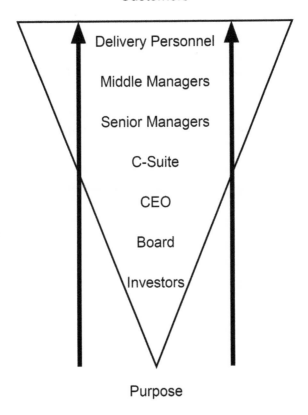

FIGURE 2 Generative Hierarchies

In a generative hierarchy, those with most accountability at the center serve those with most responsibility for customer satisfaction. Purpose aligns everyone and becomes the "boss".

Guiding *everyone* in a generative hierarchy is the purpose, which orients all towards delivering real positive impact for people and planet. This requires senior managers to make reflective and effective decisions based on business purpose, as much as profit/productivity.

But even the most generative of hierarchies will still struggle to unleash the transformational potential of people at the edges, working at the coalface, to adapt what they do in real time and solve customer needs as they emerge. Processes and procedures, and sheer human tragicomic behavior, will block adaptation and agility. To overcome this, we need something more . . . digital and disruptive.

CHAPTER 6.
FROM CHAOTIC TO CO-CREATIVE NETWORKS

The modern organization is designed for production efficiencies to increase outputs in times of stability. It is not designed for effective collaboration to solve emerging problems in times of rapid change and with the myriad complexities of our networked age. To optimize innovation and agility in a digital era, we must cultivate co-creative *networks* of cross-functional teams that deliver transformational solutions at speed, supported by a generative hierarchy.

As we enter a world of increasingly "rhizomatic" digital and physical networks, we must add to generative hierarchies a flatter, more participatory, and more decentralized organizational structure. Think circles over pyramids. Some call such network of peers of equal value and power a "heterarchy" as opposed to a hierarchy.

Such groups are composed of people who "self-organize" spontaneously to solve problems in their environment, adapt to changes they sense and see without supervision, and continue to "self-manage" themselves without the need for (much) professional oversight. Contrary to what many believe, such co-creative teams can actually be more efficient and effective than the Command and Control system.

In the 1950s, Eric Trist of the Tavistock Institute discovered that coal miners allowed to self-organize increased productivity significantly without much professional management accountability and authority. At the time, the workers challenged the Taylorist production line approach and co-created a transformational process innovation in its place. They achieved this by understanding what was needed, quite literally at the coal-face, better than the managers upstairs; and then collaborating as peers to implement it successfully together.

The Benefits of Co-Creative Networks include:

- Access more resources than any one person or enterprise can marshal alone

- Harness surges of "horizontal power" that flows through networks for movements and momentum

- Realize more diverse ideas & solutions and so lead the disruption of markets and the systemic change of systems

- Leverage future-forward insights from across the system without as much costly market intelligence and research

- Build trust, the lubrication of innovation, to ensure purposeful and profitable delivery of ambitious ideas

- Promise of faster, cheaper, better solutions with shared risks and rewards

---

Working as equals in co-creative and cross-functional teams, people can solve problems without the need for (many) managers checking for excellence, maintaining efficiency, and ensuring accountability. This is what happened at the video game company Valve: a "cabal" of peers came together in a cross-functional and co-creative team to innovate a hardware solution to user needs without management direction or systemic planning. Such self-organization and self-management could actually be our "natural" social state before dominative hierarchies evolved. How many professional managers were needed to ensure we brought down a woolly mammoth as a group?

When co-creative teams within a network are made up of people with high degrees of self-mastery and responsibility —and are supported by a generative hierarchy that prevents too much chaos and inaction— they can solve problems that matter in unprecedented ways that no single genius sitting atop a steel tower could envision. When focused through a systemic lens and inspired by a noble purpose, the diversity and openness of co-creative networks often leads to more transformational innovations than any one person (or silo) can have alone. Such innovations often have high degrees of variance to fit their complex external environment.

It is entirely likely that the urgent problems we need to solve today—from climate change and population growth to anxiety and depression—are too complex for anything other than a networked web of human hearts and minds to crack together.

When we show up as peers, valued as equal human beings (albeit with different skills and talents) rather than as job titles and pay grades, we can bring our whole self to work. This cognitive, emotional, and ethnic diversity is perhaps the greatest guard against the groupthink and groupfeel that blocks breakthroughs and trammels transformation in organizations. Networks, really do work.

Research led by sociologist of entrepreneurship Martin Ruef, then at Princeton University, demonstrated that business people with varied and rich networks are *three times more innovative* than people with predictable networks. The research was completed with elite graduates of the illustrious Graduate School of Business at Stanford University, people already known for success in value creation.

The more networked we are, the more ideas we can leverage into value-generating innovations. Little wonder that Forbes magazine has written that "according to multiple, peer-reviewed studies, simply being in an open network instead of a closed one is the best predictor of career success." Brian Eno calls the genius that emerges in a smart, and hopefully wise, network a "scenius".

Co-Creative Networks in Healthcare

'Buurtzorg' means 'neighborhood care' in Dutch. Starting out as a team of 4 nurses driven by a common purpose, the organization now has a network of 900 self-organizing co-creative teams in the Netherlands, supported by c.50 central administrators and c.20 trainers at the core. Nurses act as health coaches for patients, advising them on how to stay healthy and take care of themselves without rules from the center.

Buurtzorg has delivered savings of around 40% to the Dutch healthcare system. A case study by KMPG has found that "Buurtzorg has accomplished a 50% reduction in hours of care, improved quality of care and raised work satisfaction for their employees". This proactive process has enabled the Dutch healthcare system to reduce costs by around 40%, while the time it takes to administer care has been slashed by a staggering 50%.

When allowed to be themselves in a co-creative networks of equals, team members show up with their ideas and ideals, but also, therefore, their vulnerabilities and biases, held safe by transformational leaders who encourage safety, authenticity and evolution in a space of mutual trust, transparency and transformation. Purpose creates a strong "field" that aligns co-creative networks so they can self-organize around the right challenges without huge amounts of oversight or collaboration cost.

Even more than generative hierarchies, co-creative networks need truly conscious and empowered people within them who show up with very high levels of self-mastery. To make co-creative and cross-functional teams work without top-down management, the majority of people in the network need to be able to do what they say they will, listen and respect each other, understand what quality looks like, and have a bias towards action. Without people showing up fully with integrity, personal responsibility, and mastery of their triggers, moods, motivations, and habits, the flatness we yearn for in networks can quickly lead to a "tyranny of mediocrity" from the bottom up.

There are many well-documented and practical down-sides to such self-organizing teams that limit their effectiveness to "get stuff done" when compared to traditional hierarchies: whether compensation challenges, role proliferation or process fragmentation. Most of all, without a clear organizing principle and way to ensure wise decisions get made—that can transcend individual egos and our oxytocin-driven propensity to engage in internecine tribal warfare—things can quickly disintegrate into fractious chaos of competing desires and disunity. Think the People's Front of Judea vs. the Judean People's Front.

Perhaps the greatest challenge of flat and networked organizational structures is animosity towards any form of hierarchy at all, even generative hierarchy. When we *crave* flatness, because of an understandable distrust of dominative hierarchies, we *push* equality onto people that are not equal in talents and capabilities, leading to dysfunction and often disaster. When we unconsciously use protective patterns that we developed to resist hierarchy to force flatness on the world, we unintentionally cripple genuine co-creation.

What often happens in forcedly flat organizations is . . . very little. Co-creative energy and intentionality dissipate. There is too much debate and too many competing ideas. There is too little visionary and systemic thinking. Conflicts are not creative and constructive. Projects die due to ineffective and inefficient ways of working and weak leadership. This paralyses progress and generates a "death by consensus".

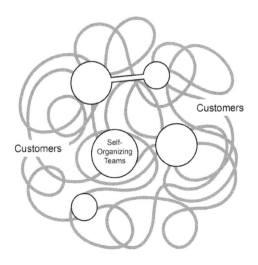

FIGURE 3 Chaotic Networks

In a chaotic network, unaware individuals come together in self-organizing and self-managing teams to serve themselve or their ideas of what will be best for the network. Goals, values, and principles are misaligned, leading to chaos and confusion.

At this moment in human evolution, I believe that many employees (and their managers) do not have the requisite levels of consciousness development to pull off truly networked, decentralized organization. Even Brian Robertson, the founder of Holocracy, has said:"[t]here is no deeper level change than this . . . [i]t requires high maturity to pull this off."

Just because we believe that all humans can be equally conscious and creative, and that we want people across the organization to be more empowered—and team members even say they want to be empowered—it still doesn't mean that everyone has the capacity or will to step-up. Some people simply don't want the added responsibilities of real decision-making power. We cannot force equality onto people that aren't ready to be fully empowered. Many people simply do not *really* want to get involved in strategic challenges, do agile innovation, or take responsibility for change—instead they want to invest their discretionary effort on hobbies, family, or community pursuits. As one HR Director we know put it: "A lot of people paid just over minimum wage don't want to be having big strategic thoughts every day."

However, it is important to realize that a lack of interest in, and capacity for, self-management and distributed leadership can also be a signal that employees, after years of being told what to do and how and when to do it, have developed "learned helplessness", like animals stuck a cage. This co-dependency on management, that often manifests as a victim/persecutor drama (with a saviour to help, as per the wonderful Drama Triangle) which tries to make the co-dependency seem "normal", can take years to transform.

Such drama and disempowerment often betrays a lack of a clear and compelling purpose in the organization and a more dominative hierarchy than people might realize. In such cases, a significant investment in energy and effort is needed to unleash the full potential of an organization to unlock the benefits of co-creative and cross-functional teams

I have witnessed many times the reality on the ground that too much self-organization and co-creation sucks up scarce time, energy, and goodwill; and so leads to poor outcomes. Research has shown that the most networked people in organizations often suffer from collaboration overload. Genuine co-creation is not always the best "mode" for delivering value to the world. Sometimes it is better to get something done quickly without debate; or even democracy.

All of this means that many companies that experiment with self-organization through purist approaches like Holocracy, often give up because the collaboration and transaction costs rise to unsustainable levels. I believe that there is actually a more fitting and adapted blueprint for organization that both transcends and includes co-creative, self-organizing, self-managing networks and prevents the chaos and instability that often comes with them. It means bringing back a little of the joys of hierarchy to help shape and support the networks, avoiding the twin specters of tyranny from the top or bottom.

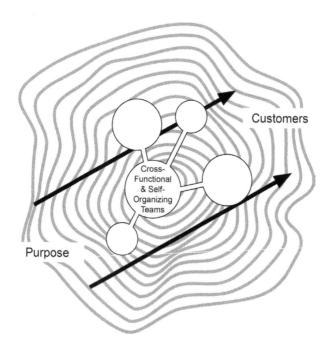

FIGURE 4 Co-Creative Networks

In a co-creative network, empowered individuals with an ownership mindset come together in self-organizing and self-managing teams to solve problems as they occur with innovation, agility, and pace. Purpose orients everyone to align goals, values, and principles; and reduce chaos and confusion.

CHAPTER 7.
THE TRANSFORMATIONAL ORGANIZATION

The constant demand for innovation, agility, and adaptation to compete in an era characterized by disruptive digital technologies, constantly changing customer needs, and existential global risks, requires leaders to transform their enterprises into Transformational Organizations that can adapt in real time to constant external pressures through innovation and change *without losing efficiency and stability*. This requires that we shift away from Command & Control by bringing together the best of generative hierarchies and co-creative networks into one organizational blueprint that is optimized for both stability and agility. I call this the Create & Control blueprint. It allows truly and constantly Transformational Organizations to be built.

The Create & Control blueprint blends the best of vertical power and network/horizontal power, linearity and non-linearity, management and leadership, control and creativity, responsibility and rights, rigid order and creative disorder, efficiency and effectiveness, and productivity and purpose. The exact combination between create and control will always have to be unique to each enterprise and its style, purpose, and history. Rather than this being an inconvenient problem, the Create & Control blueprint affords each organization the flexibility they need to architect *themselves* as to be the unique Transformational Organization they must be to fit the fast-changing world they encounter and their unique stakeholders.

In the adapatively pressured world of today, no consultancy or advisor can recommend a single solution to how a unique organization should fit the fast-moving ecology they are in, whether that means Taylorist production lines or the current vogue for matrix organization. This kind of consulting convenience is driven by exactly the old kind of linear thinking that makes organizations become maladapted in the first place.

The Transformational Organization blends together the genius of workers at the "top" and "bottom" to get what I call a "middle-out" business approach. This weaves a strong, adaptive strategic fabric out of two yarns— systemic thinkers at the "top" and agile delivery teams at the "bottom"—that are *both* elemental to the form and function of the one Transformational Organization.

Following the ancient pre-Socratic Greek philosopher Heraclitus, we bring hierarchy and heterarchy together in a "palintonic harmony". He uses the word *palintonos* to mean "that which is drawn in different directions harmonizes with itself." The Transformational Organization harmonizes the seeming opposites of control-driven and co-creative systems by blending together a generative (not dominative) hierarchy at the core and a distributed, flat(ish), and fully empowered network of cross-functional teams delivering at the edges: touchpoints of service, manufacture, and communication. Both senior leaders and cross-functional teams balance creativity with control; and adaptability with stability.

The Create & Control blueprint allows a Transformational Organization to actively and powerfully blend the opposing polarities of central/local, stable/agile, and top down/bottom up in order to design a living organizational system that harnesses the best of both worlds whilst mitigating the risks of either extreme: tyranny from above or from below. There are moments when collective sense-making and decision-making are appropriate; and there are moments where those in positions of most accountability in the generative hierarchy must step in to make fast, significant, or tough decisions to maintain quality, accountability and impact. Neither are seen as right or wrong: just different modes to fit the situation.

With the Create & Control blueprint, those in the center/ "at the top" are given permission to think systemically and strategically for the organization, always guided by an abiding and noble organizational purpose. Often with years of experience and an intellectual bent, these systemic thinkers are tasked with engaging fully in the long-term opportunities and threats of the VUCA world; and marshalling the resources needed for success in transformational change and innovation. We want them to engage with deep disruptive social drivers and the customer of the future; new exponential digital technologies; and the existential risks of a damaged planet. They provide their top-down insights, narratives, and wisdom to all, transparently.

At the same time, we also want those at the edges—at the coalface—to find and act on insights about *current* customers with agility and entrepreneurial fire. We want them to be responsive, in real time, to the reality on the ground that only they have access to. We task them to think on their feet, connect in heartfelt ways with those they serve, and feed back fresh insights from the edges to the core freely so "weak signals" can be acted upon in efficient and effective ways and transformed into exponential value-creation.

The systemic genius of senior leaders orients, enables, and inspires the activities of self-organizing teams rather than hampering it. And because those in the network step up to self-manage themselves, senior managers have more space and time to think systemically and envision long-term futures, rather than expending all their energy micromanaging people which leaves little space for major transformational thinking.

The "Create & Control" Blueprint In Multi-National Corporation Haier

Global home appliances and electronics company Haier started out as a traditional hierarchical business inspired by Taylorism. This enabled this Chinese firm to deliver quality products at scale, disrupting conventional perceptions of Chinese manufacturing prowess. To serve customer needs with more agility, the pyramid was flattened, and self-organization was promoted to enable customer pain points to be solved directly by the project's teams responsible for them.

The hierarchical pyramid was eventually inverted fully: the organization became structured around c.4000 8 member co-creative teams—or micro-enterprises—which act autonomously guided by the center (finance, HR, legal etc.). 10,000 middle managers were made redundant, empowering each team to be entrepreneurs with decision-making, recruitment and profit sharing power.

The transformation has been to maximize the value generating potential of every employee. The senior team's role is to ensure "our organization is open to outside resources", creating an ecosystem that successfully incubates innovative employee-led ideas. CEO and Chairman, Zhang Ruimin, says: "In the past, employees waited to hear from the boss; now, they listen to the customer." Haier has become the world's #1 home appliance maker with over 70,000 employees.

This blend of old and new forms is surprisingly transformative and unleashes everyone to be their best without tying everyone's hopes to an idealistic vision that is not realizable in practice. I have worked *really* hard to empower tens of thousands of mid-level and junior employees across multi-national corporations and huge national public entities. My experience tallies with the groundbreaking work of Catherine Turco at MIT: many people want—and probably at this stage of our social and cultural evolution, still need—a bit of old-fashioned control and management accountability with their co-creation and shared responsibility.

Too much chaos creates panic, fear, and overwhelm in the brain and body, which leads to survival responses that diminish capacity and lessen the quality of outcomes. Neuro-biologically, people feel safe with the clarity and order that comes from lite and supple management practices that can be designed for generative hierarchies. I believe that most employees want the openness, transparency, and democracy of co-creative cross-functional teams when they feel "held" by senior leaders who support them; and ensure all feel "psychologically safe".

In an organization premised on a Create & Control blueprint, everyone honors the need to "Get Stuff Done" efficiently with low transaction costs and without lots of needless variation, debate, and creativity. Yet everyone also embraces the need to regularly open up dialogue and decision-making to all, so that the organization can adapt strategies and tactics in real time; generate innovations out of fresh future-forward insights gleaned at the coal-face when serving customers; and collectively find ways to bring the purpose to life for all stakeholders.

In this model, neither those nominally at top or bottom are judged as more or less valuable as human beings. All are seen as essential parts of the organizational system with equal inherent worth. Neither group are subservient to the other. In fact, both serve the purpose rather than heroic leaders, shareholders, or union bosses. As decentralized management pioneer Tom Thomison says: "Purpose is the boss!"

As a corollary of blending together hierarchy with networks, the nature of the roles and responsibilities human beings have within Transformational Organizations change substantially. After centuries of prioritizing technical expertise within tightly defined job roles (e.g. Market Analyst or Product Manager)—with people incentivized to become brilliant at one tiny area of human knowledge and practice (in effect, the PhD model)—we will certainly see a shift towards the value of generalists who can adapt to perform well in many roles; and can adapt and evolve the roles themselves.

People must be able to elegantly transfer their wisdom and smarts to solve new, adapative and transformational problems within new roles. This is happening already. Deloitte predicts that within a decade, 70% to 90% of workers will be in such multivalent roles or "superjobs". Like a form of quantum superposition, they must be ready to pivot their skills and approaches to solve new challenges at will and in an instant—without resistance or reluctance.

In predictable and stable environments, "rules"— encoded in best practice and procedures / policies developed over the lifetime of a business)—ensure risks are minimized and outputs maximized. But in the rapidly changing VUCA context, old rules are often maladapted to emergent realities. Then best practice starts to kill the"next-practice" that the organization needs to stay fitted with customers and technology. Expertise, when applied without wisdom, blocks the disruptive innovation and transformation that an organization needs to survive and thrive in the fast-moving ecosystem.

This is challenging. A 2015 study from Yale found that the more senior leaders invest in building and iterating their systems of knowledge—(AKA the rules)—the harder they find it to unlearn their expertise and so allow transformation to occur. When senior leaders in a dominative hierarchy are too attached to their industry expertise and those below are unable to effectively challenge assumptions with fresh (user-focused) insights, it leaves the organization locked into old business models and ways of working that eventually lead to corporate death. Locking rules into roles within a dominative hierarchy is therefore very dangerous. Generative hierarchies that allow co-creative and self-managing teams to operate within them guard against this groupthink and groupfeel by allowing those with next-practice to share it without being shot down or dimished by vertical (or "old") power.

The need for constant role adaptation is accerated by AI and automation, which will (soon!) be able to handle even nonroutine analytical tasks better than human beings (without bias, fatigue etc). This will leave human workers the exciting challenge of engaging with *unanticipated* problems: which most often need divergent, creative solutions not just the application of old rules from within old roles. This means their role will adapt as they think and act, not before hand with perfect planning from HR. It also means the people doing the job as it evolves will be best placed to define the roles as they unfold. Create & Control systems allow this crucially adapative learning and development to occur at the edges and be codified back within the core of the generative hierarchy.

An interesting possibility is that every major function within an organization might work best when split into two equal roles: one person acts as a guardian of "control", ensuring stability, efficiency and order; and another acts as a guardian of "create", like innovation, adaptation, and agility. There is a possibility that one person, who has mastered both mindsets, could do both roles (I do as the founder of Switch On). This echoes the transformational power of a great COO and CEO partnership. There is also an interesting, although dangerous, precedent for this in the design of the USSR's Red Army, which vanquished the German Wermacht before the Western Allies did: a military commander in charge of operations paired with a political officer in charge of "morale" (this is not to say the Red Army was anything like an empowering Transformational Organization).

In a Create & Control blueprint, those "below" are able to surface assumptions and unlock the rule-book whilst those "at the top" no longer have to have expertise in every domain and be "the best" at everything the organization does. Senior managers are still able to use their wisdom and expertise to rein in excessive creativity and adaptability if it starts to threaten stability. *All* are empowered to evolve their thinking and skills to serve emerging roles and problems.

The "Create & Control" Blueprint In Civil Society Organizations: The National Rifle Association and Black Lives Matter

The NRA and BLM, unbelievably different civil society organizations that exist on diametrically-opposed polarities of the socio-political spectrum in the USA, share major similarities in how they organize which has allowed them to mobilize the vertical and horizontal power of hundreds of thousands of citizens. This has made them two of the most important social movements in US history.

The NRA, whilst it has encountered a number of scandals and setbacks of late, has a fiersome central core that develops profoundly systemic thinking and orchestrates collective action: lobbying powerful lawmakers, keeping key messages in the public eye, and constantly shaping the debate to focus on rights and liberties rather than the 40,000 tragic deaths per year from guns. At the same time, the NRA funds scores of ideas and initiatives at the edges, driven by distributed leaders across the USA. The NRA brings the ideas that strike a chord or are exponentially impactful to the core to be scaled.

Black Lives Matter, started by a handful of women, is a fully distributed organization that balances a little central systemic innovation (developing toolkits, memes, and other resources) with lots of network / horizontal power. With over 40 local chapters, transformational energy surges through the communities where change needs to happen. BLM was the first human rights movement in US history to successfully use "mediated mobilization" to get people moving. As they say on their website: "To maximize our movement muscle, and to be intentional about not replicating harmful practices that excluded so many in past movements for liberation, we made a commitment to placing those at the margins closer to the center."

In a Create & Control blueprint, risks are shared between the nominal top and bottom. Therefore, I believe that rewards must be too. However, this sharing of wealth and power has to happen without us losing the benefits of the "high peaks" of creativity, vision, and determination of ambitious and entrepreneurial people. Inequality of pay can therefore be reduced whilst still rewarding those with flair and ambition for their efforts. Ownership and remuneration flattens out towards the edges, just as power does in digital networks.

The Create & Control blueprint, therefore, provides us a very concrete opportunity to recalibrate the global balance between social classes without violence, agitation, or repression. This can allow "capital" and "labor" to work together respectfully to solve problems that really matter to all. We can harness the Create & Control blueprint to repair and regenerate the corroding social contract in advanced liberal democracies and usher in an age of what I call "Connected Capitalism".

I sense that this will have a marked impact on the political instability and social turbulence that is driving the world to the brink of conflict; and allow the coming shocks of the climate crisis and techonological alienation (from AI and robots) to be engaged in by all without us losing it all.

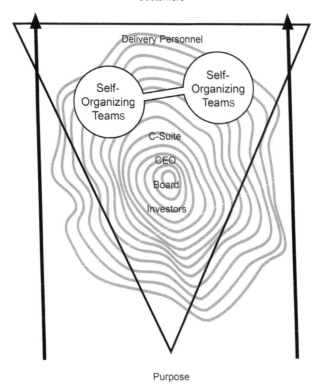

FIGURE 5 Create & Control: Co-Creative Networks Working Within A Generative Hierarchy.

Self-organizing teams solve problems and make change at the edges; whilst systemic thinkers engage in strategic transformation at the core. Accountable leaders ensure compliance, ethics, and integrity across the organization by inspiring, empowering, and serving those on the frontlines. Purpose orients everyone and is the boss.

CHAPTER 8.
CREATE & CONTROL SYSTEMS

Having transformed the overall form and function of the modern organization so it can be both agile and stable, let's drill down to the detail to see how things change compared to the conventional Command & Control archetype. This is all emergent thinking as my team and I support the design and build of Create & Control systems in real time with our clients to generate truly Transformational Organizations:

Overall Goals

To constantly adapt products, processes, and people to positively transform the lives of users delivering purpose (concrete beneficial impact for all stakeholders) and profit in a sustainable way by galvanizing the agility and creativity of self-organizing networks of empowered employees without losing the stability of generative hierarchy and the strategic and systemic capabilities of senior managers.

Value Creation

The organization seeks to deliver excellent customer value in the short-term *and* generate long-term exponential value within regenerative "planet-positive" business models. Digital technologies are leveraged with fresh insights into emerging users in disrupted societies to solve problems that really matter within the damaged world. Value is delivered through ecosystems of trusted collaborators with each partner playing to their strengths.

Ownership & Financial Returns

Risks, and so rewards, are shared between investors and employees (and sometimes users). Those with more ambition and effort perform more systemic and strategic roles and are rewarded for this to a reasonable degree with a limit to the income multiple of senior managers vs. delivery employees.

Accountability & Authority

Appropriate success criteria and KPIs for projects are co-created by cross-functional teams of equals coached by senior managers. KPIs shift significantly depending on whether agility/innovation or stability/improvement outcomes are being prioritized. The entire team is accountable for delivery; and all employ self-management to drive performance. Authority for budgets and decisions is shared between those in management roles and those in delivery roles. The more people across the organization take on radical responsibility, the more authority is spread from the conventional "top" to "bottom". Teams decide reward/corrective measures, coached by senior managers.

Visual Metaphor

An inverted pyramid with senior managers and shareholders serving those on the front lines—and self-organizing and cross-functional teams in circles/networks co-creating, co-delivering, and co-learning to deliver ever-improving value for purpose and profit.

Roles

Transparent roles and "role principles" are co-created by managers and teams and are adapted and evolved *in real time* in response to changes in the environment to maximize the delivery of profit *and* purpose. People are encouraged to take on new roles; and to upgrade their existing roles to align with their passions, talents, and purpose. People move from being technical experts within a functional role to becoming generalists with many roles, aided by technology. Roles can be shared and adapted as individuals and teams grow and change.

Responsibilities

Psychological safety and mutual trust encourage personal responsibility-taking and resultant rapid learning. Responsibility is seen as empowering, creative, and transformational not moral.

Guidance & Decision-Making

Transparent principles are co-created by cross-functional teams to inform how people should think and act in appropriate and legal ways. People are trusted to interpret these principles, and evolve them when needed, to make specific decisions in the moment. "Mistakes" are explored for learnings for the individual, the team, and the organization as a whole. This allows "failures" and "issues" to be harnessed for "double-loop" organizational learning and so accelerated innovation/transformation.

Processes

Lean processes for key outcomes are co-designed by cross-functional teams coached by senior managers. They are upgraded regularly (but not too regularly); and are designed around real humans (customers, users, vendors). Processes are designed to be the Minimum Viable Structure neccesary for successful outcomes on purpose and profit; and to utilize technology to free up human capacities for innovation/transformation.

Key Activities

Manage the existing business efficiently with evolving best-practice at the same time as leading strategic innovation/transformation effectively to invent next-practice. Efficiency and technology upgrades are deployed to reduce costs where appropriate and emerging science/technologies are explored to transform business models. HR/IT/Finance (etc.) specialists co-create solutions within cross-functional teams.

Innovation

Systemic, rigorous, strategic, purpose-driven, and transformational innovation is led in collaborations between senior managers at the core and cross-functional teams at the edge. Rapidly deployed incremental and evolutionary innovations are led by self-organizing delivery teams with coaching/inspiration/input from senior managers.

Motivational Levers

Focus on intrinsic motivation to generate shared responsibility and mutual trust with meaning (purpose, fulfilment), mastery (autonomy, growth), and membership (belonging, community). Extrinsic motivation harnessed for more transactional outcomes.

Culture

Transformational mindsets (including the embrace of uncertainty, smart experimentation, and deep human insight) and a "fail-forward" learning culture open up constant opportunities for positive change and innovation. Personal responsibility-taking allows excellent peformance. Leaders, at the top and in teams, are afforded the time, space, and permission needed to sense weak signals, reflect on behaviors and assumptions, and experiment to forge next-practice.

Diversity

Encouragement of cognitive, emotional, gender, and ethnic diversity—and appropriate and healthy debate.

Information Flow

Conditions are created for timely, empowered, and creative dialogues with a bias towards full transparency. Communications flow to/from senior managers and cross-functional teams without fear, distortion, or dominance so information is accurate and can be acted upon appropriately.

Leadership

Leadership is distributed across teams to serve the purpose, not hierarchical power. Leaders harness transformational, inspirational, and conscious leadership styles to effect transformation with minimal resistance. They focus on developing their wisdom, storytelling, and systemic change skills to embrace creativity at the "edge of chaos" whilst "holding space" for team members to focus on delivery in an atmosphere of safety, common purpose, mutual trust, and shared responsibility. Senior managers do not need to know more than smart technical experts.

Coaching & Empowerment

Straight yet compassionate feedback and a coaching style are encouraged across the organization (I.e. from below and above) without losing the value of boundaries, accountability, and discomfort. Complaining, shaming, and blaming is actively transformed into empowerment and ownership. Management conversations (improvements based on poor outcomes) and coaching conversations (genuine empowerment for the sake of the individual) are actively distinguished.

Organizing Principles

The organization is seen as a complex, adaptive, living system with human beings collaborating together in cross-functional teams that evolve and adapt in real time to fit outside-in changes; and solve emerging challenges. Mechanistic/linear thinking, algorithmic processes, and machine learning are employed to automate tasks and drive efficiencies without ever assuming the real world is linear. This allows human beings to focus on caring (about users and impact), creativity, and collaboration. Intuition and insight are valued as much as data and knowledge; and data is used for creativity and emancipation as much as control.

Underlying Assumptions About Human Nature

People are inherently capable, willing, and trustworthy. When inspired by a genuine purpose within a culture cultivated for creativity and empowerment, they can create extraordinary results without (much) supervision and with minimal control. Everyone has the same inherent value.

CHAPTER 9.
THE SCIENTIFIC EVIDENCE BEHIND THE
CREATE & CONTROL BLUEPRINT

The evidence from history, biology, and the social sciences shows that the philosophers Thomas Hobbes and Jean-Jacques Rousseau were both right: we need strong yet generative hierarchies to guard against our darker shadows, to promote safety and ethical behaviors, and to make tough decisions that protect people. But we also need to engage all citizens as equals, to connect with open hearts and open minds in order to create solutions to our most challenging problems together. There is increasing evidence that organisms, organizations, and societies that can exist in a generative tension between control and creativity, between top-down and bottom-up, are best adapted to the trials and tribulations of today. Here is a brief review of some key thinking from across human knowledge:

EVIDENCE FROM NEUROSCIENCE, AI & BIOLOGY

The last decade of neurobiology suggests that there are two key Modes—associated with specific brain networks—that drive leadership and organizational behavior. In Control & Protect Mode, associated with the Executive Control Network, people are goal-directed, convergent, focused, traditionally smart, happy to work alone, and guided by best practice. This is the Mode associated with conventional management that organizations use, to be efficient. However, this Mode is poor at adapting to fast-changing environments and is not very successful at collaboration. We also have another Mode, Create & Connect Mode, associated with the Default Mode Network, in which we are imaginative, divergent, open, wise, collaborative, and able to invent next-practice. We are able to solve new problems in new ways and have high levels of empathy to enable us to co-create with others.

The latest neuroscience fMRI research has shown that these networks are usually operating antagonistically. For example, when the executive network is activated, the default network is usually deactivated. Yet highly innovative people are able to rapidly cycle between create and control capabilities. The complex process of imagining and executing high-value new ideas—whether everyday adaptation and agility of long-range transformational innovation—involves a complex interplay between creative and controlled thinking. The Create & Control Organizations, mirror the way our brain networks work together in a palintonic harmony to engage in *both* divergent *and* convergent thinking.

Pioneering neuroscientist and psychiatrist Iain McGilchrist studies the hemispheric specialization of the human brain. He has discovered through brain scans and lesion studies, that the right hemisphere engages in the whole and the left hemisphere focuses on the parts. One side has evolved for holistic, systemic and often imaginative ways of thinking. One side for focused, task-specific detailed ways of thinking. The corpus callosum, which connects the two hemispheres, also separates them: a crucial function that allows their highly evolved and valuable processing styles to operate without risk that their distinct ways of engaging in reality will be flattened or nullified. The Create & Control organization likewise allows for the crucial separation of Create & Control approaches, honoring both as adaptively vital to surviving and thriving.

The top-down and bottom-up "middle-out" operating model of the Create & Control blueprint can be glimpsed in emerging theories of neurological cognition, like that proposed by UCLA psychiatrist and theorist Dan Siegel. These suggest that we think through a cognitive symphony of top-down, "higher" cognitive functions in the cerebral cortex and bottom-up, "lower" interoceptive information from the body, viscera and senses. The brain matches predictions about how the world should be with information from the senses about how it actually is. According to a leading expert in emotions, Professor Lisa Feldman Barrett, it is dissonance between top-down predictions and bottom-up sensibilities that creates much of our emotional states in a form of "middle-out" processing.

Unsurprisingly then, recent advances in Artificial Intelligence have been predicted on deep learning through neural networks that mirror this middle-out cognitive strategy. They take in information from the bottom up and compare it with hypotheses generated at the top. In cutting-edge AI, "General Adversarial Networks" generate predictions about how reality should look (e.g. the shape of a cat) and then examines incoming data to see if it fits these expectations. The AI learns about the world through a middle-out process of creativity (hypotheses, theory and prediction) and then taking in inputs from how things actually are and "fact checking" them, updating the theory as they go (control). This is similar to how the scientific method works in practice.

Research from cell biology shows that even the most basic biological organisms need a cell membrane. Otherwise they die. A cell needs to be a coherent whole that can *control* the influx and excretion of materials and protect itself from threats. But if that membrane is not semi-permeable—to allow in fresh resources (ideas and insights in organizations) from the network / ecosystem—the cell also dies. An organism needs to be responsive and adapt as well as controlling to survive and thrive. Interestingly, if such cell membranes were not able to connect to other membranes, we'd still be single cell amoebas incapable of forming more complex organizing structures, like the human brain or a global multi-national.

Research from primate studies and biological anthropology has shown that humans are without doubt the most co-operative and co-creative species in the primate world. This capacity for co-creation is vital to our ability to colonize the planet. Harvard's Professor Richard Wrangham has studied humankind for decades and believes that our cooperation skills are equally important to our capacities for physical power and violent control to our success as a species. In other words, we have developed highly-tuned create and control capabilities that can be used to survive to pass on our genes; and thrive as we live, love and lead in our lives.

EVIDENCE FROM THE SOCIAL SCIENCES

Research by archaeologists and anthropologists has shown that pre-modern societies have either evolved the hierarchical model, which inevitably becomes dominative with a bias towards violence and oppression; or a flatter "partnership" model, driven by trusted linkages and connective relationships rather than by command and control, that has led to much more peaceful, sustainable, and collaborative societies. Riane Eisler proposes, in her book *The Chalice and the Blade*, that—despite cultural narratives normalizing Western dominative hierarchies— we are not doomed to exist within systems of authority and abuse. We can reclaim and reinvent the partnership model, which has deep roots in earlier forms of culture such as the thriving society of Minoan Crete.

Contemporary sociology and social psychology have also posited that there is a global tension between control and create, between protect and connect, and between hierarchy and partnership, with every culture and country somewhere on the continuum. Psychology professor Michele Gelfand's research studied 33 national cultures and found that how "tight" or "loose" they are, determines the capacity to change of that society or sub-culture. How loose or tight is in large part down to how much threat (natural or social) a society has faced or perceives they face.

Recent scholarship has attempted to understand what has worked or not in the last 60 years of social change movements which have all attempted to rewire society from within. There are some clear lessons from organizations as diverse as Mothers Against Drunk Driving and the National Rifle Association: systemic organizational hierarchy with top-down accountability and impact must be balanced with local chapters activating people at the edges to support the movement and be the change. The key reason that both the Arab Spring and Occupy Wall Street movements failed to land sustainable transformation is that they suffered from too much networked co-creativity and not enough systemic control (from within a generative hierarchy). Both need to be poised in a creative tension for the best results.

When a society gets the palintonic harmony between create and control right, innovation blooms. This appears to account for the huge flowering of civic and cultural innovation seen in ancient Athens that has so influenced our modern world. As Stanford historian Josiah Ober points out in his book *The Rise and Fall of Classical Greece*, in centralized systems, rulers "determine who does what in the production of goods and who gets what in the distribution . . . wealth and power are concentrated at and distributed by the center." In contrast, the "Greek miracle" was in part a result of decentralized, networked cooperation with distributed innovation and investment. Ober believes that the greatest achievement of Athens was to bring people together in a cohesive and coherent whole (i.e. an organization) without erasing the differences between them through standardization or domination.

CHAPTER 10.
METRICS AND MOTIVATION IN THE TRANSFORMATIONAL ORGANIZATION

Key to the success of the The Transformational Organization is to use metrics when they are useful in optimizing outcomes and improving efficiency; whilst realizing that metrics can only measure some elements of material change and often pervert purposeful behavior when used indiscriminately. By the same token, we must understand that extrinsic motivations like promotion and bonuses are sometimes useful in creating momentum; yet the returns have been shown to diminish quickly so we should focus predominately on building intrinsic motivations like meaning, mastery, and membership that can be sustained long-term.

METRICS

Metrics are powerful ways of measuring what has and what hasn't occurred in the material world. They can ensure that we understand exactly what is occurring in the constellation of activities that make up a business with clarity and transparency. As such, they are an essential element for optimizing our outcomes, whether led by a senior leader within a generative hierarchy or enacted by self-managing individuals within a network. Data gives us useful information with which to make business decisions and to hold ourselves, and others, accountable.

However, in the last few decades, metrics have been created as proxies for just about every goal and purpose. Examples from across government, business, schools and healthcare, have shown that the pursuit of the improvement of metrics often fails to lead to improvements in the actual outcomes that are desired. Measuring Math and English scores as a proxy for overall learning, and then rewarding and punishing teachers based on those metrics, has actually led to less positive outcomes for children and society. Incentivizing employees with quotas has led to unethical mis-selling, fraud, and huge fines for companies like Wells Fargo. Managing hospital performance with metrics has led to patients being left in ambulances, new and needless roles being created, and providers refusing to treat difficult cases so as not to reduce their metrics.

Management science generated in the Industrial Age to increase performance on production lines cannot be used in *all* human systems to drive the most meaningful and valuable outcomes at all times. Perverse outcomes like those above occur in part because the metrics chosen are often poor proxies for the purposeful goals of the organization. Also the penalties and incentives that are put in place around the metrics then disturb the inherent motivation of people to achieve that purpose rather than amplify it. In dominative hierarchies, performance management has become a way to punish rebels and cajole slackers rather than empower and enable people to step up. Employees, feeling untrusted and disrespected, react by gaming the system, cheating, and resisting. This perpetuates the class warfare between labor and capital.

Metrics are important for measuring manufacturing statistics, some customer and employee activities, and interactions with software of any kind. As such they are elemental for the "control" element of the Create & Control system. The more a task is simple, repetitive, instrumental and directly productive, the better a metric fits for managing outputs and outcomes. If the drive to achieve the task is already reliant on external motivation, such as a bonus based on sales or downloads, then managing performance using the metric can be helpful. It may still be a poor proxy for actual purposeful outcomes, such as client satisfaction or consumer app usage, but it may enable the amplification of effort and focus in a non-alienating way.

However transformational leaders must always be aware that many metrics are not great proxies for the intended aims of an organization and that poorly designed metrics and performance management approaches often lead to unintended consequences that damage the organization's purpose and fabric. "Rule cascades" are often instituted as organizations try to solve faulty metrics, creating treacle-like processes and procedures that cause immense friction and block the "create" element necessary for organizational adaptability and agility. So, when tasks are complex, purposeful, unique, and driven by intrinsic motivators—such as going out of the way to delight customers or driving forward a breakthrough innovation—then metrics are poor ways to measure performance. If the metrics are perceived by committed employees as inappropriate or misleading, the more they will game, ignore, or resist them.

MOTIVATION

Senior leaders and self-managing team leaders in a Transformational Organization must understand whether a task is more likely to be driven by an internal or external motivation. Traditional economic thinking is premised on the idea that human beings always respond to extrinsic incentives: money, fame, a gold watch etc. Yet psychologists and sociologists have shown in study after study that rewards and punishments are often counterproductive because they undermine *intrinsic* motivations.

Intrinsic motivations are the sense of mastery we feel when we nail something after growing as people to achieve it; the sense of membership we feel as part of a team working on something of value and relevance, and the sense of meaning we have when we co-create positive impact for people with purpose. When nurtured and cultivated, they remain strong no matter how adverse external conditions get. Whereas external motivators like "incentives are . . . only weak re-enforcers in the short run, and negative re-enforcers in the long run." Even if designed with an open heart, extrinsic motivators eventually exhaust their power, demanding new rules and rewards to be invented.

Rules and rewards (of any kind) are extrinsic motivators. They shape behavior in a coarse way. They hold people accountable but often with a sense of violence. Rules and rewards often corrode the drive we all have within to do things well for ourselves and humankind. They can alienate us from ourselves and from the culture we are part of. The impact of this can be seen in blood-bank research in Israel: rewarding donors financially for giving blood actually reduces the amount of blood donated. It creates a financial metric as a proxy for something done because of care, compassion, and purpose. The extrinsic incentive undermined the responsibility-taking of the donors.

Taking responsibility for a purposeful outcome, because we genuinely care, is perhaps the strongest of intrinsic motivators. So, when we generate a purpose that travels through a generative hierarchy from bottom to top and pervades a network like a magnetic field, we align the most powerful intrinsic motivator of everyone in the organization. Then we are fully accountable not simply because a manager measures our performance indicators but because we truly want to be, because it is why we exist. Then performance indicators, co-designed by ourselves and our manager, help all understand what is happening and how we can adjust to improve; but we never mistake the map for the territory, the metrics for our intrinsic motivation and worth.

CHAPTER 11.
BIO-TRANSFORMATION THEORY

I have spent 20+ years discovering and refining a theory of transformation (of individuals and organizations) and a methodology for leading desired transformations that we have come to call Bio-Transformation Theory. It is grounded in the very latest science, particularly the neuroscience of human biology (all transformation must occur in warm and wet neurons first and foremost); and the science of complex, living adapative systems. The "bio" in Bio-Transformation Theory (BTT) means "life" or "living". These disciplines, as well as the behavioral sciences and psychological sciences, attempt to create certain knowledge about how things really work "out there", in brain cells, social dynamics, and ecological systems.

However, Bio-Transformation Theory is also rooted in the world's great philosophical traditions, which have spent thousands of years trying to understand the internal, subjective experience of being human; and how to change that experience through choosing to feel, think and act differently. Bio-Transformation Theory painstakingly blends these two great rivers together—mapping scientific facts, paper by paper, to wise insights, text by texts—whilst making it all uber-useful by drawing on practical tools and techniques from areas like coaching, entrepreneurship, and behavioral economics (like "nudge" tools).

Proven by over 100 successful projects and programs—and working with over 100,000 individuals in cultures across the globe —BTT has never failed to deliver exponential solutions (breakthroughs that could not have been predicted by extrapolating the past) to emerging and challenging adaptive problems. It can be trusted to provide the right structures and spaces for an organization to lead and land continuous transformations and constant adaptations without falling into disarray and chaos. It combines a linear, controllable convergent process with necessary non-linear, creative divergence. Therefore it can allow leaders to manage existing business and operating models efficiently whilst leading the creation of future business and operating models effectively.

Underlying BTT is The Transformation Curve, which I believe to be nature's blueprint for all transformations, whether in the biology of individual employees and leaders or paradigm shifts complex, adaptive systems such as your organization and the ecosystem it relies on for sustenance. The Transformation Curve maps how humans biologies and people-populated systems move from mismatched, outdated solutions (whether internal processes or external products) to future-positive, planet-ready solutions as effectively and efficiently as possible.

By leading ourselves and others across The Transformation Curve, we build new and more appropriate "higher-level" orders that include and build upon the old order; but have new emergent properties within them that fit the changing world better. This allows us to not only survive evolutionary pressures but to metabolize them into value as we adapt, grow, and so thrive because of them. We can, if we follow the logic of The Transformation Curve, wrestle from the jaws of chaos fundamental breakthroughs in people, products, and processes.

BTT as a whole ensures we heed the evolutionary imperative to "adapt or die". In organizational systems, we can use it to shift organizational processes, procedures, and structures by allowing senior leaders and employees to co-design the transformations themselves. People like me act as guides, process experts, and tool providers. BTT allows us to transcend yet include hierarchy and control to find a higher-order sense of organizational cohesion and individual meaning that equips us to deal with the "Triple Threat" admirably. More than this, it allows us to turn them into a "Triple Opportunity" by conscious choice.

I hope and believe that more and more C-Suite leaders will realize that the old linear and silo-ed ways of managing change, executing innovation, doing organizational restructuring, and developing talent are failing. Study of The Transformation Curve suggests that it is inevitable that the pain of fading and failing will eventually move many leaders to seek such genuine and continuous transformation to ensure that their organization stays match fit to survive in the ever-more digital, disrupted, and damaged world.

However, a warning for those that wait to hit rock-bottom when the (hostile) take-over bids are coming in or the bankruptcy proceedings have been filed: The Transformation Curve tells us that at this point, there is usually no longer enough time, energy, trust, or goodwill to make it across the Transformation Curve. Just ask Kodak, Blockbuster, or Nokia.

To make it simple, as legendary CEO Jack Welch said: "Change before you have to."

CHAPTER 12.
KEY PRINCIPLES FOR BECOMING A
TRANSFORMATIONAL ORGANIZATION

1. Turning your enterprise into a Transformational Organization cannot, and must not, happen overnight. Gone are the days when a single linear Industrial-Age change initiative, restructure or I.T roll-out can deliver the transformation needed in the Digital Age. Instead, organizations must "build the plane whilst they are flying it": engaging in continuous future-forward transformation systematically, strategically, and systemically whilst ensuring business-as-usual continues without fail(s).

2. Break out of the cycle of change programs being cascaded down from the top on long-suffering employees only to peter out in time for the next one. Instead lead and empower all to be the change themselves: refining and rewiring processes internally and products externally so they serve the future, not the past.

3. This is an evolutionary journey that will never be "finished" like a traditional restructure or "reorg". It is a transformation path to ensure your organization can constantly realize its full potential to adapt with agility and pace to seize the exponential opportunities of the digital, disrupted, and damaged world—whilst mitigating the many risks of under-performance, irrelevance, and obsolescence.

4. There is no one-size-fits-all solution. Every organization has a different business model, history and culture and so what is right for one will not be right for another. Instead, the principles of The Transformational Organization must be interpreted into your organization as you architect a structure that blends the right amount of create vs. control.

5. Consultants do not have all the answers. Leaders must resist the temptation to outsource their adaptation challenges to management consultants that themselves rely on outdated Industrial-Age management thinking. Management consultants and process engineers will never understand the culture and ways of working in a client enterprise as much as those inside. And because transformation needs to be continuous, organizations must build capacity within to be able to do it constantly. It is neither economical nor practical to have external consultants lead constant change. They are easy to hire and easy to blame which all too often pushes ownership of the transformation to those who do not have the power necessary to lead it and land it.

6. The journey of empowering your people to be truly transformational, balancing creativity with control, starts by unleashing your own people's insights and ideas about how to become a Transformational Organization. It is essential to start to build serious muscle in non-linear transformation now, as you will be invited by the fast-changing world to transform again and again in the coming decades.

7. Be prepared to invest for exponential returns. The rewiring of an organization to become transformational cannot be done on the cheap. It will take a sustained investment of time, energy, and resources. Do not do it if you are not committed as it gets people's hopes up only to disappoint them again. Trust that the value-created will be an exponential Return On Investment because your teams will be able, willing, and ready to invent the future of your organization and industry not just once but many times.

8. Start small but hold a big vision for a truly transformational organization. Imagine a bold vision for how your organization can reinvent itself to be adaptable yet stable. But then start the transformation process in one area of the organization, with a handful of cross-functional teams. Use transformational innovation best practice to prototype rapidly, fail small and fast, and learn quickly before you evolve, scale and mainstream. Use systems thinking to find "sweet spots" where small changes could

create outsized positive outcomes. Go for quick yet significant wins to build confidence and trust.

9. Sense into what is happening now *before* you make big changes. Sense-make collectively *before* you design and act. Begin by listening and learning from everyone, understanding where the organizations is currently at, where the lines of power and accountability interact, where processes are ill-adapted to the environment, where the greatest pain and suffering is, and where people are not agile, empowering, and creative.

10. Mindsets must transform *before* the structures, processes, and strategies transform. Organizations cannot embed a transformational way of doing business into their organization without changing the hearts and mindsets of the people in the organization. The "immune system" of the Command & Control approach will attempt to shut down attempts at transformation in products, processes and people (whether called "innovation", "digital transformation", "culture-change" or anything else) until the DNA of the organization, and so its immune system, is rewired one leader and one employee at a time.

11. Mindsets and habits—like micromanaging, needing to be the smartest in the room, acting disempowered, or creating victim/persecutor dramas—must change otherwise resistance will hold everything back. This can be very challenging for most people, including

leaders at the very top, who must unlearn old habits, rules, and beliefs or they will hold back the organization.

12. The foundational shift to a Create & Control model requires that leadership development no longer happens in classrooms. Instead it must act as crucial on-the-job support for delivering transformational innovation outcomes on tangible and concrete problems—whilst still giving leaders space, time, and permission to reflect and connect.

13. Empower *all* employees to become transformational, not just those in the C-Suite. Obviously this cannot be done if human development in organizations remains itself locked into the Industrial-Age model. The Transformational Organization seeks to unleash the potential of all to be able to effect change, at whatever scale. All must be empowered to expand their palettes of responses to everyday challenges to ensure the organizations has the requisite variety needed to survive and thrive in the digital, disrupted, and damaged world.

14. Ensure processes and digital technologies are updated to support adaptability and stability. Processes usually work best when they are designed in co-creation between those who actually have to do the work along with experts with vision and systemic insight. Incorporate digital technologies, including AI and automation, slowly and always to

solve concrete problems as they emerge—rather than jumping on costly bandwagons that do not have a clear purpose or value.

15. Learn from, and adapt, existing technologies rather than immediately buying complex I.T systems for digital transformation. License, borrow, and improve open-source technologies, self-management processes, agile and scrum methods, lean techniques, social technologies like Slack, decision-making tools like Loomio, design thinking and disruptive innovation practices and more to fast-track the transformation. Customized systems can always be generated once the prototypes and hacks have been tested. Don't stay purist to any one approach. A combination of clear principles and a bricolage of hacks and fixes are better than a "perfect" but inflexible solution.

16. Use the transformation journey to embed a massive upgrade in your leadership, team, and innovation capacity. This shift to a Transformational Organization is a perfect way to move towards a more creative, transformational, and agile culture. Harness the process to up-skill emerging talent so they can do strategic innovation; and to up-skill senior leaders so they can lead people to transform.

17. Bring together those that "own" organization design/ change/development, talent/people, structure, operations, business models, strategy and innovation

at the top to share their budgets and their brilliance and deliver the full weight of their systemic vision. They must work together to drive forward culture change, leadership, strategy, and innovation *all at the same time*. Silos and fiefdoms have to break down at the top first to allow others to co-create powerful solutions.

18. Senior executives must recognize something they don't teach on MBAs: whoever shapes the people and culture of an organization to become transformational owns the keys to the kingdom of future success.

19. Ultimately, a small group of transformational leaders in the existing hierarchy have to switch on and step up to change how change is done. They must give up seeking safe, linear, and incremental Industrial-Age solutions to complex, fast-evolving, network-driven "transformational problems"—and be ready to guide and cultivate non-linear transformational solutions that fit the digital, disrupted, and damaged era we are in.

CHAPTER 13.
CONCLUSIONS

» Every enterprise faces a fundamental challenge that is key to its short-term survival and long-term thriving: how to organize itself to meet the intense and unprecedented demands of the 21st Century VUCA reality (characterized by exponential digital technologies, disrupted societies, and the existential risks of a damaged world).

» Organizations need to have a level of creativity and responsiveness within them that matches the variety found in the outside world (the market). Organizations that do not have high levels of agility and adaptability rapidly become maladapted and fail.

» Today, and in future, transformation must be continuous because the world is changing continuously. Just like technology, companies launch their products in "continuous beta", organizational transformation can no longer be conceived as a project but an approach to doing business.

» Organizations urgently need to unlock the transformational potential of their people, to adapt fast enough to fit the outside world.

» Most leaders meet the urgent need for increased agility and adaptability by tweaking the edges of the traditional Command and Control model. These efforts inevitably fail because this underlying Industrial-Age blueprint for organization was partly designed to crush such initiatives. The DNA of the modern organization evolved to limit the very innovation, empowerment, self-organization, and agility now needed to survive and thrive in the fast-changing Digital Age.

» Every organization must reinvent itself as a Transformational Organization: one that can continuously metabolize changes in the outside world into concrete value within its business models and operating models.

» Some brave organizations are attempting to become transformational by experimenting with self-management approaches such as "Holocracy" and "Teal". However, the increased collaboration costs and chaos they often bring usually undermine the benefits; and we doubt their capacity to enact truly transformational innovation.

» The "Create & Control" system blueprint allows organizations to become transformational by blending the benefits of a generative, rather than dominative, hierarchy (senior managers, leveraging systemic vision and transformational innovation, support and serve those delivering for customers); and the benefits of co-creative networks (where self-organizing and self-motivating teams work to adapt at the front lines, with agility).

» The Create & Control blueprint affords organizations the greatest chance of being able to continuously transform themselves safely, systemically, strategically, and systematically to stay relevant as times change. It unleashes the adaptability needed to incorporate exponential technologies into solving unmet customer needs whilst tethering the organization and its people with the stability needed to turn such transformational innovations into commercially-viable and planet-positive business models.

» The Create & Control model affords genuinely new *ways of working* and roles that can adapt as times change that enable it to constantly bring in new insights, value-creating ideas, and exponential technologies into the processes and products through which it solves customer problems and serves customer needs; whilst at the same time maintaining the accountability and reliability necessary to deliver on customer, investor, and employee expectations for predictability and stability.

» The Create & Control blueprint also has the potential to renew the social contract of liberal democracy between workers and managers and thus transcend the political crises, inequalities, and demagogueries of the age.

» By harmonizing profits and performance with purpose and potential, the Create & Control blueprint allows enterprise to attract and retain the most transformational talent by meeting their existential demands for three key intrinsic motivators: meaning, mastery, and membership.

» The Transformational Organization realizes that business-as-usual must be re-wired to afford continuous adaptation *without descending into too much chaos*—which endangers the enterprise and exhausts the employees. The Transformational Organization must be able to strategically move from order into disorder, systematically de-constructing existing processes and products with planned disruption "at the edge of chaos", before moving back to a higher degree of order that leads to more employee, enterprise, and ecosystem thriving. You must be able to take things apart without falling apart, on an everyday basis.

» There is no one-size-fits-all solution to the successful transition to a Transformational Organization built upon a Create & Control blueprint. Instead, each enterprise must go on their own journey to architect and implement a version that fits their industry, culture, capabilities, resources, history, ambition, strategy, and purpose. Bio-Transformation Theory and practice can ensure that this journey is successful.

FREE READER OFFER:
10-DAY EMAIL COURSE

As a valued reader, we are offering you a free 10-day email course to explore some of the core principles of Transformational Leadership.

You'll get your free PDF when you sign up to our mailing list at **http://www.switchonnow.com/bto**

You will also receive invites to read future books on transformation in business in advance of publication.

ABOUT SWITCH ON

Switch On is a transformation company working in organizational, leadership, and personal development with a global reputation for transformational leadership development, transformational change, and transformational innovation programs. Our programs and products ensure enterprises forge the future of the digital, disrupted, and damaged world—rather than fail it.

Switch On is a purpose-driven organization that seeks to spread the critical philosophies, methods, tools and practices of Bio-Transformation Theory to communities of leaders, that can affect global systemic change. Switch On has worked with C-Suite levels leaders of organizations such as Kellogg's, Intel, Genentech, HSBC, Unilever, Oxfam, WWF, NHS, UK Civil Service, Innovate UK, and many more.

SELECTED BIBLIOGRAPHY

Acs, Audretsch, Acs, Zoltan J, & Audretsch, David B. (2010). *Handbook of Entrepreneurship Research : An Interdisciplinary Survey and Introduction* (2nd ed., International Handbook Series on Entrepreneurship ; 5). New York, NY: Springer New York : Imprint: Springer.

Alexander, L. (2017) This Is The Mind-Set You'll Need In Order To Thrive In The Future Of Work. *Fast Company* blog 3 July. Available at: https://www.fastcompany.com/3068725/this-is-the-mind-set-youll-need-to-thrive-in-the-future-of-work (Accessed 20 March 2019).

Amabile, T and Kramer, S J. (2011) The Power of Small Wins. *Harvard Business Review,* May 2011. Available at: https://hbr.org/2011/05/the-power-of-small-wins (Accessed 20 March 2019).

Anderson, C. and Brown C. E. (2010) Research in Organizational Behaviour. *Berkeley EDU* article 2010. Available at https://www.haas.berkeley.edu/faculty/papers/anderson/functions%20and%20dysfunctions%20of%20hierarchy.pdf (Accessed 20 March 2019).

Argyris, C. (1999). On organizational learning (2nd ed.). London: Blackwell.

Beaty, R. (2018) Why Are Some People More Creative Than Others? *Scientific American* blog 16 January. Available at: https://www.scientificamerican.com/article/why-are-some-people-more-creative-than-others/ (Accessed: 20 March 2019).

Beaty, R. E. et. al. (2018) Beaty, R., Kenett, Y., Christensen, A., Rosenberg, M., Benedek, M., Chen, Q., . . . Silvia, P. (2018). Robust prediction of individual creative ability from brain functional connectivity. *Proceedings of the National Academy of Sciences of the United States of America*, 115(5), 1087-1092.

Benabou, R., & Tirole, J. (2003) Intrinsic and Extrinsic Motivation. *Review of Economic Studies*, 70, pp. 489–520.

Bernstein, E. et al (2016) Beyond the Holacracy Hype. *Harvard Business Review blog* July/August. Available at: https://hbr. org/2016/07/beyond-the-holacracy-hype (Accessed: 20 March 2019).

Cilliers, Paul, 2001. Boundaries, Hierarchies and Networks in Complex Systems. *International Journal of Innovation Management*, 5(2), pp.135–148.

Cook, G. (2018) 'A Powerful Force That Shapes All of our Decisions', Scientific American blog 11 September. Available at: https:// www.scientificamerican.com/article/a-powerful-force-that-shapes-all-of-our-decisions/ (Accessed: 20 March 2019).

Cross, R and Rebele, R and Grant, A. (2016) 'Collaborative Overload', Harvard Business Review blog January/February. Available at: https://hbr.org/2016/01/collaborative-overload (Accessed 20 March 2019).

Crutchfield, L. R. (2018). *How Change Happens: Why Some Social Movements Succeed While Others Don't* (1 edition). Wiley.

Eisler, R. (1995) *The Chalice and the Blade: Our History, Our Future*. San Francisco: Harper & Row.

Feldman Barrett, L. (2015), 'The Predictive Brain', edge.org., Available at: https://www.edge.org/annual-question/2016/ response/26707 (Accessed: 7 March 2019).

Fisher, M. & Keil, F. C., 2016. The Curse of Expertise: When More Knowledge Leads to Miscalibrated Explanatory Insight. *Cognitive Science*, 40(5), pp.1251–1269.

Freinacht, H. (2017) 'What Is The Model of Hierarchical Complexity?', Metamoderna blog, 8 September 2017. Available at http://metamoderna.org/what-is-the-mhc?lang=en (Accessed: 20 March 2019).

Fry, D. (2013). *War, Peace, and Human Nature: the Convergence of Evolutionary and Cultural Views*. New York: Oxford University Press.

Harford, T. (2014) When metrics make for desperate measures. Available at: https://www.ft.com/content/444b6ea2-0043-11e8-9650-9c0ad2d7c5b5 (Accessed: 7 March 2019).

HBR's 10 Must Reads Big Business Ideas Collection (2015-2017)

Jankel, N. (2018) 'The Future Of Business: How Enterprises Can Thrive In A Digital, Disrupted & Despairing World', Medium blog January. Available at: https://medium.com/swlh/the-future-of-business-how-enterprises-can-thrive-in-a-digital-disrupted-despairing-world-7084d32aec68 (Accessed: 20 March 2019).

Kohlberg, L. (1984). *The psychology of moral development : The nature and validity of moral stages.* (Essays on moral development ; v.2). San Francisco ; London: Harper & Row.

Konner, M. (2019) A Bold New Theory Proposes That Humans Tamed Themselves. *The Atlantic*, March. Available at: https://www.theatlantic.com/magazine/archive/2019/03/how-humans-tamed-themselves/580447/ (Accessed: 7 March 2019).

Lahey, L. and Kegan, R.. (2016). *An Everyone Culture: Becoming a Deliberately Developmental Organization*. Harvard University Press

Laloux, F. (2004) *Reinventing Organizations: A Guide to Creating Organizations Inspired by the Next Stage in Human Consciousness.* Brussels: Nelson Parker.

Lamport Commons, Michael. (2014). Introducing a new stage for the model of hierarchical complexity: A new stage for reflex conditioning. *Behavioral Development Bulletin*, 19(3), 1-9.

Levinson, M. (2017) '*The Whole Story of Holacracy at Blinkist*', Medium blog 6 April. Available at: https://medium.com/key-lessons-from-books/the-whole-story-of-holacracy-65ec6bc855c3 (Accessed 20 March 2019).

McGilchrist, I. (2009) *The Master and His Emissary: The Divided Brain and the Making of the Western World.* London: Yale University Press.

McNamara, C. (2012) '*Consulting and Organizational Development*', Free Management Library blog 26 June. Available at: https://managementhelp.org/blogs/consulting-skills/2012/06/26/history-of-organization-development-part-5-of-6-—-wilfred-bion-and-eric-trist-the-birth-of-self-managed-work-groups/ (Accessed 20 March 2019).

Mankins, M. (2007) Reduce Organizational Drag. *Harvard Business Review*, 2 March 2017. Available at: https://hbr.org/ideacast/2017/03/globalization-myth-and-reality-2.html (Accessed: 20 March 2019).

Marinatos, N. (1993). *Minoan religion: Ritual, image, and symbol.* Columbia, SC: University of South Carolina Press.

Michael Keaton McDonald's Franchise (2016) *THE FOUNDER Official Trailer.* Available at https://www.youtube.com/watch?v=VBIxg3XiBaw (Accessed: 20 March 2019).

Naughton, J. (2017) What scientific term or concept ought to be more widely known? *Edge 2017.* Available at: https://www.edge.org/response-detail/27150 (Accessed: 20 March 2019).

Ogilvy, J. (2016) Heterarchy: An Idea Finally Ripe for Its Time *Forbes blog 4 February.* Available at: https://www.forbes.com/sites/stratfor/2016/02/04/heterarchy-an-idea-finally-ripe-for-its-time/#3df9a9c247a7 (Accessed: 20 March 2019).

Robertson, B. J. (2016). *Holocracy: The Revolutionary Management System that Abolishes Hierarchy.* Penguin

Ronfeldt, D. (1996) *Tribes, Institutions, Markets, Networks: A Framework About Societal Evolution.* Santa Monica, CA: RAND Corporation. Available at: https://www.rand.org/pubs/papers/P7967.html. Also available in print form.

Ruef, M. (2010) Let a Hundred Flowers Blossom: The Cross-Fertilization of Organization Studies at Stanford, *The Sociology of Organizations* 28, pp. 387-393.

Ruskin, John. (1905). *Unto this last.* London: George Allen.

Seligman, M., & Beagley, G. (1975). Learned helplessness in the rat. Journal of Comparative and Physiological Psychology, 88(2), 534-541.

Siegel, D J. (2016), 'The open mind', *Aeon blog* 24 October. Available at https://aeon.co/essays/how-the-old-and-the-new-make-the-mind-ebb-and-flow (Accessed: 20 March 2019).

Simmons, M. (2015) The No. 1 Predictor Of Career Success According To Network Science. *Forbes* blog, 15 January. Available at: https://www.forbes.com/sites/michaelsimmons/2015/01/15/this-is-the-1-predictor-of-career-success-according-to-network-science/#507d1d8de829 (Accessed: 7 March 2019).

Sterling, B. (2008) Scenius, or Communal Genius. *Wired* Blog 16 June. Available at: https://www.wired.com/2008/06/scenius-or-comm/ (Accessed 20 March 2019).

The Guardian (2019) *UK wages worth up to a third less than in 2008*. Available at https://www.theguardian.com/business/2018/dec/14/average-uk-worker-earn-third-less-than-2008-tuc-real-wage-report?CMP=Share_iOSApp_Other (Accessed: 20 March 2018).

Trist, E. (1989). *The Assumptions of Ordinariness as a Denial Mechanism: Innovation and Conflict in a Coal Mine*. Human Resource Management, 28(2), 253.

Tufekci, Z.: Twitter and Tear Gas: The Power and Fragility of Networked Protest: Yale University Press, 2017.

Turco, C J. (2016), 'Can Conversation Supplant Bureaucracy?', Strategy and Business blog 19 October. Available at: https://www.strategy-business.com/article/Can-Conversation-Supplant-Bureaucracy?gko=613b1 (Accessed: 20 March 2019). https://encode.org (2019) (Accessed: 20 March 2019).

Tyano, S., Munitz, H., & Wijsenbeek, H. (1975) 'Psychological and sociological aspects of blood donation in Israel', Revue française de transfusion et immuno-hématologie, 18 (3), pp. 326-32.Scott D. A, et. al. (2018) "2018 Corporate Longevity Forecast: Creative Destruction is Accelerating" Available at https://www.innosight.com/insight/creative-destruction/ (Accessed: 20 March 2018).

Vedantam, S. (2019) The Hidden Brain: One Head, Two Brains: How The Brain's Hemispheres Shape The World We See [Podcast]. 4 February. Available at: https://www.npr.org/2019/02/01/690656459/one-head-two-brains-how-the-brains-hemispheres-shape-the-world-we-see?t=1551115244967&t=1551974725142 (Accessed: 7 March 2019).

Vlassopoulos, K. (2016) 'Bryn Mawr Classical Review', BMCR blog 4 March. Available at: http://bmcr.brynmawr.edu/2016/2016-03-04.html (Accessed: 20 March 2019).

Volini, E. et. al. (2019) 'From jobs to superjobs', 2019 Global Human Capital Trends, Deloitte Insights, April. Available at: https://www2.deloitte.com/insights/us/en/focus/human-capital-trends/2019/impact-of-ai-turning-jobs-into-superjobs.html (Accessed: 7 June 2019).

Vozza, S. (2017) 'Why Employees At Apple And Google Are More Productive', Fast Company blog, 13 March. Available at: https://www.fastcompany.com/3068771/how-employees-at-apple-and-google-are-more-productive (Accessed: 7 March 2019).

West, Geoffrey. *Scale: The Universal Laws of Growth, Innovation, Sustainability, and the Pace of Life, in Organisms, Cities, Economies, and Companies.* Penguin Pr. May 2017. 496p. illus. notes. index. ISBN 9781594205583. $30; ebk. ISBN 9781101621509. SCI

Wikipedia (2018) 'The Organization Man', Wikipedia, 4 December 2018. Available at: https://en.wikipedia.org/wiki/The_Organization_Man (Accessed: 20 March 2019).

Wikipedia (2019) 'Lawrence Kohlberg's stages of moral development', Wikipedia, 13 February 2019. Available at: https://en.wikipedia.org/wiki/Lawrence_Kohlberg%27s_stages_of_moral_development (Accessed 20 March 2019).

Wrangham, R. (2019) The Goodness Paradox: How Male Resentment Created Tolerance, Morality and Homo Sapiens. London: Profile Books.